50 The Best Pie Recipes

By: Kelly Johnson

Table of Contents

- Classic Apple Pie
- Pumpkin Pie
- Pecan Pie
- Cherry Pie
- Blueberry Pie
- Key Lime Pie
- Chocolate Cream Pie
- Lemon Meringue Pie
- Sweet Potato Pie
- Peach Pie
- Strawberry Rhubarb Pie
- Coconut Cream Pie
- Banana Cream Pie
- Shoofly Pie
- Maple Cream Pie
- Blackberry Pie
- Raspberry Pie
- Fig Pie
- Chocolate Peanut Butter Pie
- Sour Cherry Pie
- Mince Pie
- Cranberry Pie
- Caramel Apple Pie
- S'mores Pie
- Chess Pie
- Buttermilk Pie
- Apple Crumble Pie
- Strawberry Pie
- Almond Cream Pie
- Mincemeat Pie
- Bourbon Pecan Pie
- Nutella Pie
- Lemon Chess Pie
- Caramelized Pear Pie
- Mixed Berry Pie
- Pear Ginger Pie

- Pumpkin Praline Pie
- Cream Cheese Pumpkin Pie
- Apple Cranberry Pie
- Spiced Pear Pie
- Chocolate Silk Pie
- Chocolate Hazelnut Pie
- Pineapple Pie
- Apricot Pie
- Coconut Lime Pie
- Grapefruit Pie
- Maple Pecan Pie
- Mocha Cream Pie
- Apricot Almond Pie
- Plum Pie

Classic Apple Pie

Ingredients:

- 2 1/2 lbs apples (Granny Smith or Honeycrisp), peeled, cored, and sliced
- 1/4 cup granulated sugar
- 1/4 cup brown sugar, packed
- 1 tbsp lemon juice
- 1 tsp ground cinnamon
- 1/4 tsp ground nutmeg
- 2 tbsp all-purpose flour
- 1/2 tsp vanilla extract
- Pinch of salt
- 1 package of refrigerated pie crusts (or homemade pie crusts)
- 1 tbsp butter, cut into small pieces

Instructions:

1. Preheat the oven to 425°F (220°C).
2. In a large bowl, combine the apples, sugars, lemon juice, cinnamon, nutmeg, flour, vanilla extract, and salt.
3. Roll out one pie crust and fit it into a 9-inch pie pan.
4. Pour the apple mixture into the pie crust and dot with butter.
5. Roll out the second pie crust and place it over the apples. Trim excess dough and crimp the edges to seal.
6. Cut slits in the top crust to allow steam to escape.
7. Bake for 45-50 minutes, until the crust is golden brown and the filling is bubbly.
8. Let the pie cool before serving.

Pumpkin Pie

Ingredients:

- 1 can (15 oz) pumpkin puree
- 3/4 cup granulated sugar
- 1 tsp ground cinnamon
- 1/2 tsp ground ginger
- 1/4 tsp ground nutmeg
- 1/4 tsp ground cloves
- 1/2 tsp salt
- 3 large eggs
- 1 can (12 oz) evaporated milk
- 1 tsp vanilla extract
- 1 refrigerated pie crust (or homemade pie crust)

Instructions:

1. Preheat the oven to 425°F (220°C).
2. In a large bowl, whisk together the pumpkin, sugar, spices, and salt.
3. Add the eggs and beat until smooth.
4. Gradually stir in the evaporated milk and vanilla extract.
5. Pour the mixture into the pie crust.
6. Bake for 15 minutes, then reduce the temperature to 350°F (175°C) and bake for another 40-45 minutes, until the filling is set.
7. Let the pie cool completely before serving.

Pecan Pie

Ingredients:

- 1 1/2 cups pecan halves
- 3/4 cup corn syrup
- 1/2 cup granulated sugar
- 1/2 cup brown sugar, packed
- 1/4 cup unsalted butter, melted
- 3 large eggs, lightly beaten
- 1 1/2 tsp vanilla extract
- 1/4 tsp salt
- 1 9-inch pie crust (store-bought or homemade)

Instructions:

1. Preheat the oven to 350°F (175°C).
2. In a large bowl, whisk together corn syrup, granulated sugar, brown sugar, melted butter, eggs, vanilla extract, and salt.
3. Stir in the pecans.
4. Pour the mixture into the prepared pie crust.
5. Bake for 50-60 minutes, until the pie is set and golden brown on top.
6. Let the pie cool completely before slicing and serving.

Cherry Pie

Ingredients:

- 4 cups fresh or frozen cherries
- 1 cup granulated sugar
- 2 tbsp cornstarch
- 1 tbsp lemon juice
- 1/4 tsp almond extract (optional)
- 1/4 tsp vanilla extract
- Pinch of salt
- 1 package of refrigerated pie crusts (or homemade pie crusts)

Instructions:

1. Preheat the oven to 375°F (190°C).
2. In a saucepan, combine cherries, sugar, cornstarch, lemon juice, almond extract (if using), vanilla extract, and salt.
3. Cook over medium heat, stirring occasionally, until the mixture thickens and becomes bubbly.
4. Roll out one pie crust and fit it into a 9-inch pie pan.
5. Pour the cherry mixture into the pie crust.
6. Roll out the second pie crust and place it over the cherries. Trim excess dough and crimp the edges to seal.
7. Cut slits in the top crust to allow steam to escape.
8. Bake for 45-50 minutes, until the crust is golden brown.
9. Let the pie cool before serving.

Blueberry Pie

Ingredients:

- 4 cups fresh or frozen blueberries
- 1 cup granulated sugar
- 1/4 cup cornstarch
- 1 tbsp lemon juice
- 1/4 tsp ground cinnamon
- Pinch of salt
- 1 package of refrigerated pie crusts (or homemade pie crusts)

Instructions:

1. Preheat the oven to 375°F (190°C).
2. In a large bowl, combine blueberries, sugar, cornstarch, lemon juice, cinnamon, and salt.
3. Roll out one pie crust and fit it into a 9-inch pie pan.
4. Pour the blueberry mixture into the pie crust.
5. Roll out the second pie crust and place it over the blueberries. Trim excess dough and crimp the edges to seal.
6. Cut slits in the top crust to allow steam to escape.
7. Bake for 45-50 minutes, until the crust is golden brown.
8. Let the pie cool before serving.

Key Lime Pie

Ingredients:

- 1 can (14 oz) sweetened condensed milk
- 1/2 cup fresh lime juice
- 2 large egg yolks
- 1 package of graham cracker crust (store-bought or homemade)
- Lime zest, for garnish

Instructions:

1. Preheat the oven to 350°F (175°C).
2. In a bowl, whisk together sweetened condensed milk, lime juice, and egg yolks until smooth.
3. Pour the mixture into the graham cracker crust.
4. Bake for 10-12 minutes, until set but still jiggly in the center.
5. Let the pie cool to room temperature, then refrigerate for at least 2 hours.
6. Garnish with lime zest before serving.

Chocolate Cream Pie

Ingredients:

- 1 pre-baked pie crust (store-bought or homemade)
- 1 cup heavy cream
- 1/2 cup whole milk
- 3/4 cup granulated sugar
- 1/4 cup unsweetened cocoa powder
- 3 tbsp cornstarch
- 1/2 tsp vanilla extract
- 3 oz semi-sweet chocolate, chopped
- Whipped cream, for topping

Instructions:

1. In a saucepan, whisk together milk, cream, sugar, cocoa powder, and cornstarch.
2. Cook over medium heat, stirring constantly, until the mixture thickens and comes to a simmer.
3. Remove from heat and stir in chopped chocolate and vanilla extract.
4. Pour the filling into the pre-baked pie crust and smooth the top.
5. Refrigerate for at least 2 hours, until set.
6. Top with whipped cream before serving.

Lemon Meringue Pie

Ingredients:

- **For the filling:**
    - 1 1/2 cups water
    - 1 cup granulated sugar
    - 1/4 cup cornstarch
    - 1/4 tsp salt
    - 4 large egg yolks, beaten
    - 1/2 cup fresh lemon juice
    - 2 tbsp unsalted butter
    - 1 tsp lemon zest
- **For the meringue:**
    - 4 large egg whites
    - 1/4 tsp cream of tartar
    - 1/2 cup granulated sugar
- 1 pre-baked pie crust

Instructions:

1. Preheat the oven to 350°F (175°C).
2. In a saucepan, combine water, sugar, cornstarch, and salt.
3. Cook over medium heat, stirring constantly, until thickened.
4. Gradually add the beaten egg yolks, whisking constantly.
5. Stir in lemon juice, butter, and lemon zest.
6. Pour the filling into the pre-baked pie crust.
7. In a separate bowl, beat egg whites and cream of tartar until soft peaks form.
8. Gradually add sugar and beat until stiff peaks form.
9. Spread the meringue over the lemon filling, sealing the edges.
10. Bake for 10-12 minutes, until the meringue is golden.
11. Let the pie cool completely before serving.

Sweet Potato Pie

Ingredients:

- 2 cups cooked sweet potatoes, mashed
- 1/2 cup granulated sugar
- 1/4 cup brown sugar, packed
- 1/2 tsp ground cinnamon
- 1/2 tsp ground nutmeg
- 1/4 tsp ground ginger
- 1/2 tsp vanilla extract
- 2 large eggs
- 1/2 cup evaporated milk
- 1/4 cup unsalted butter, melted
- 1 pre-baked pie crust

Instructions:

1. Preheat the oven to 350°F (175°C).
2. In a bowl, combine mashed sweet potatoes, sugar, brown sugar, cinnamon, nutmeg, ginger, vanilla extract, eggs, evaporated milk, and melted butter.
3. Mix until smooth.
4. Pour the mixture into the pre-baked pie crust.
5. Bake for 45-50 minutes, until the filling is set.
6. Let the pie cool before serving.

Peach Pie

Ingredients:

- 4 cups fresh or frozen peaches, peeled and sliced
- 1 cup granulated sugar
- 2 tbsp cornstarch
- 1 tbsp lemon juice
- 1/4 tsp ground cinnamon
- Pinch of salt
- 1 package of refrigerated pie crusts (or homemade pie crusts)

Instructions:

1. Preheat the oven to 375°F (190°C).
2. In a large bowl, combine peaches, sugar, cornstarch, lemon juice, cinnamon, and salt.
3. Roll out one pie crust and fit it into a 9-inch pie pan.
4. Pour the peach mixture into the pie crust.
5. Roll out the second pie crust and place it over the peaches. Trim excess dough and crimp the edges to seal.
6. Cut slits in the top crust to allow steam to escape.
7. Bake for 45-50 minutes, until the crust is golden brown and the filling is bubbly.
8. Let the pie cool before serving.

Strawberry Rhubarb Pie

Ingredients:

- 3 cups fresh rhubarb, chopped
- 3 cups fresh strawberries, hulled and sliced
- 1 1/2 cups granulated sugar
- 1/4 cup cornstarch
- 1/4 tsp salt
- 1 tbsp lemon juice
- 1 package of refrigerated pie crusts (or homemade pie crusts)

Instructions:

1. Preheat the oven to 375°F (190°C).
2. In a large bowl, combine the rhubarb, strawberries, sugar, cornstarch, salt, and lemon juice.
3. Roll out one pie crust and fit it into a 9-inch pie pan.
4. Pour the fruit mixture into the pie crust.
5. Roll out the second pie crust and place it over the fruit. Trim excess dough and crimp the edges to seal.
6. Cut slits in the top crust to allow steam to escape.
7. Bake for 45-50 minutes, until the crust is golden brown and the filling is bubbling.
8. Let the pie cool before serving.

Coconut Cream Pie

Ingredients:

- 1 pre-baked pie crust (store-bought or homemade)
- 2 cups whole milk
- 1 cup heavy cream
- 3/4 cup granulated sugar
- 1/4 cup cornstarch
- 1/4 tsp salt
- 3 large egg yolks, lightly beaten
- 1 tsp vanilla extract
- 1 1/2 cups shredded sweetened coconut
- 1/2 cup whipped cream (for topping)

Instructions:

1. In a medium saucepan, combine milk, cream, sugar, cornstarch, and salt.
2. Cook over medium heat, whisking constantly, until the mixture thickens.
3. Gradually whisk in the egg yolks and cook for another 2-3 minutes.
4. Remove from heat and stir in vanilla extract and shredded coconut.
5. Pour the coconut filling into the pre-baked pie crust.
6. Let the pie cool to room temperature, then refrigerate for at least 2 hours.
7. Top with whipped cream before serving.

Banana Cream Pie

Ingredients:

- 1 pre-baked pie crust (store-bought or homemade)
- 2 cups whole milk
- 1/2 cup granulated sugar
- 1/4 cup cornstarch
- 1/4 tsp salt
- 3 large egg yolks, lightly beaten
- 1 tbsp unsalted butter
- 1 tsp vanilla extract
- 3 ripe bananas, sliced
- 1/2 cup whipped cream (for topping)

Instructions:

1. In a medium saucepan, combine milk, sugar, cornstarch, and salt.
2. Cook over medium heat, whisking constantly, until the mixture thickens.
3. Gradually whisk in the egg yolks and cook for another 2-3 minutes.
4. Remove from heat and stir in butter and vanilla extract.
5. Let the filling cool slightly, then pour it into the pre-baked pie crust.
6. Layer the banana slices on top of the filling.
7. Refrigerate for at least 2 hours.
8. Top with whipped cream before serving.

Shoofly Pie

Ingredients:

- 1 pre-baked pie crust (store-bought or homemade)
- 1 1/2 cups all-purpose flour
- 1 cup packed brown sugar
- 1 tsp baking soda
- 1/2 tsp ground cinnamon
- 1/2 tsp salt
- 1/2 cup unsalted butter, softened
- 1 cup molasses
- 1 large egg, beaten
- 1 cup hot water
- 1/2 tsp vanilla extract

Instructions:

1. Preheat the oven to 375°F (190°C).
2. In a bowl, combine flour, brown sugar, baking soda, cinnamon, and salt.
3. Cut in the butter until the mixture resembles coarse crumbs.
4. In a separate bowl, whisk together molasses, egg, hot water, and vanilla extract.
5. Pour the molasses mixture into the dry ingredients and stir until combined.
6. Pour the filling into the pre-baked pie crust.
7. Bake for 40-45 minutes, until the filling is set.
8. Let the pie cool before serving.

Maple Cream Pie

Ingredients:

- 1 pre-baked pie crust (store-bought or homemade)
- 1 cup maple syrup
- 1/2 cup heavy cream
- 3 large egg yolks
- 1 tbsp unsalted butter
- 1 tsp vanilla extract
- 1/4 tsp salt
- 1/2 cup whipped cream (for topping)

Instructions:

1. In a medium saucepan, combine maple syrup and heavy cream.
2. Heat over medium heat until the mixture begins to simmer.
3. In a bowl, whisk together egg yolks and vanilla extract.
4. Gradually add the hot syrup mixture into the egg yolks, whisking constantly.
5. Return the mixture to the saucepan and cook over low heat, stirring constantly, until it thickens.
6. Remove from heat and stir in butter and salt.
7. Pour the filling into the pre-baked pie crust.
8. Refrigerate for at least 2 hours before serving.
9. Top with whipped cream before serving.

Blackberry Pie

Ingredients:

- 4 cups fresh or frozen blackberries
- 1 cup granulated sugar
- 1/4 cup cornstarch
- 1 tbsp lemon juice
- 1/4 tsp ground cinnamon
- Pinch of salt
- 1 package of refrigerated pie crusts (or homemade pie crusts)

Instructions:

1. Preheat the oven to 375°F (190°C).
2. In a large bowl, combine blackberries, sugar, cornstarch, lemon juice, cinnamon, and salt.
3. Roll out one pie crust and fit it into a 9-inch pie pan.
4. Pour the blackberry mixture into the pie crust.
5. Roll out the second pie crust and place it over the blackberries. Trim excess dough and crimp the edges to seal.
6. Cut slits in the top crust to allow steam to escape.
7. Bake for 45-50 minutes, until the crust is golden brown and the filling is bubbling.
8. Let the pie cool before serving.

Raspberry Pie

Ingredients:

- 4 cups fresh or frozen raspberries
- 1 cup granulated sugar
- 1/4 cup cornstarch
- 1 tbsp lemon juice
- Pinch of salt
- 1 package of refrigerated pie crusts (or homemade pie crusts)

Instructions:

1. Preheat the oven to 375°F (190°C).
2. In a large bowl, combine raspberries, sugar, cornstarch, lemon juice, and salt.
3. Roll out one pie crust and fit it into a 9-inch pie pan.
4. Pour the raspberry mixture into the pie crust.
5. Roll out the second pie crust and place it over the raspberries. Trim excess dough and crimp the edges to seal.
6. Cut slits in the top crust to allow steam to escape.
7. Bake for 45-50 minutes, until the crust is golden brown and the filling is bubbling.
8. Let the pie cool before serving.

Fig Pie

Ingredients:

- 2 cups fresh figs, chopped
- 1 cup granulated sugar
- 1/4 cup cornstarch
- 1 tbsp lemon juice
- 1/4 tsp ground cinnamon
- Pinch of salt
- 1 package of refrigerated pie crusts (or homemade pie crusts)

Instructions:

1. Preheat the oven to 375°F (190°C).
2. In a large bowl, combine figs, sugar, cornstarch, lemon juice, cinnamon, and salt.
3. Roll out one pie crust and fit it into a 9-inch pie pan.
4. Pour the fig mixture into the pie crust.
5. Roll out the second pie crust and place it over the figs. Trim excess dough and crimp the edges to seal.
6. Cut slits in the top crust to allow steam to escape.
7. Bake for 45-50 minutes, until the crust is golden brown and the filling is bubbling.
8. Let the pie cool before serving.

Chocolate Peanut Butter Pie

Ingredients:

- 1 pre-baked pie crust (graham cracker or chocolate)
- 1 cup peanut butter
- 8 oz cream cheese, softened
- 1 cup powdered sugar
- 1 cup whipped cream
- 1 cup semi-sweet chocolate chips
- 1 tbsp unsalted butter

Instructions:

1. In a bowl, combine peanut butter, cream cheese, and powdered sugar.
2. Mix until smooth and fluffy.
3. Fold in whipped cream until well combined.
4. Pour the peanut butter mixture into the pie crust.
5. In a microwave-safe bowl, melt chocolate chips and butter together. Stir until smooth.
6. Pour the chocolate over the peanut butter filling and spread evenly.
7. Refrigerate for at least 2 hours before serving.

Sour Cherry Pie

Ingredients:

- 4 cups fresh or frozen sour cherries
- 1 cup granulated sugar
- 1/4 cup cornstarch
- 1 tbsp lemon juice
- 1/4 tsp almond extract (optional)
- 1 package of refrigerated pie crusts (or homemade pie crusts)

Instructions:

1. Preheat the oven to 375°F (190°C).
2. In a large bowl, combine cherries, sugar, cornstarch, lemon juice, and almond extract.
3. Roll out one pie crust and fit it into a 9-inch pie pan.
4. Pour the cherry mixture into the pie crust.
5. Roll out the second pie crust and place it over the cherries. Trim excess dough and crimp the edges to seal.
6. Cut slits in the top crust to allow steam to escape.
7. Bake for 45-50 minutes, until the crust is golden brown and the filling is bubbling.
8. Let the pie cool before serving.

Mince Pie

Ingredients:

- 2 1/2 cups mincemeat (store-bought or homemade)
- 1 package of refrigerated pie crusts (or homemade pie crusts)
- 1 tbsp brandy or rum (optional)
- 1/2 tsp ground cinnamon
- 1/4 tsp ground nutmeg
- 1/4 tsp ground cloves

Instructions:

1. Preheat the oven to 375°F (190°C).
2. Roll out one pie crust and fit it into a 9-inch pie pan.
3. Fill with mincemeat, and sprinkle with cinnamon, nutmeg, and cloves.
4. Roll out the second pie crust and place it over the mincemeat. Trim excess dough and crimp the edges to seal.
5. Cut slits in the top crust to allow steam to escape.
6. Bake for 45-50 minutes, until the crust is golden brown.
7. Let the pie cool before serving.

Cranberry Pie

Ingredients:

- 2 cups fresh cranberries
- 1 cup granulated sugar
- 2 eggs, beaten
- 1/2 cup unsalted butter, melted
- 1/2 cup flour
- 1/2 tsp vanilla extract
- 1/4 tsp salt
- 1 pre-baked pie crust (store-bought or homemade)

Instructions:

1. Preheat the oven to 375°F (190°C).
2. In a bowl, mix together cranberries, sugar, eggs, melted butter, flour, vanilla, and salt.
3. Pour the cranberry mixture into the pie crust.
4. Bake for 40-45 minutes, until the filling is set and slightly golden on top.
5. Let the pie cool before serving.

Caramel Apple Pie

Ingredients:

- 6 cups apples, peeled and sliced
- 1 cup granulated sugar
- 1 tbsp lemon juice
- 1 tsp ground cinnamon
- 1/4 tsp ground nutmeg
- 1 tbsp cornstarch
- 1/2 cup caramel sauce (store-bought or homemade)
- 1 package of refrigerated pie crusts (or homemade pie crusts)

Instructions:

1. Preheat the oven to 375°F (190°C).
2. Toss the sliced apples with sugar, lemon juice, cinnamon, nutmeg, and cornstarch.
3. Roll out one pie crust and fit it into a 9-inch pie pan.
4. Pour the apple mixture into the pie crust and drizzle with caramel sauce.
5. Roll out the second pie crust and place it over the apples. Trim excess dough and crimp the edges to seal.
6. Cut slits in the top crust to allow steam to escape.
7. Bake for 50-60 minutes, until the crust is golden brown and the filling is bubbling.
8. Let the pie cool before serving.

S'mores Pie

Ingredients:

- 1 pre-baked graham cracker pie crust
- 2 cups semi-sweet chocolate chips
- 1/2 cup heavy cream
- 1 cup mini marshmallows
- 1 tbsp unsalted butter
- 1 tsp vanilla extract

Instructions:

1. Preheat the oven to 350°F (175°C).
2. In a saucepan, heat heavy cream and butter over medium heat until it starts to simmer.
3. Remove from heat and stir in the chocolate chips and vanilla extract until smooth.
4. Pour the chocolate mixture into the graham cracker crust.
5. Top with mini marshmallows.
6. Bake for 10-15 minutes until the marshmallows are golden brown.
7. Let the pie cool before serving.

Chess Pie

Ingredients:

- 1 pre-baked pie crust (store-bought or homemade)
- 1 1/2 cups granulated sugar
- 1 tbsp cornmeal
- 1 tbsp all-purpose flour
- 1/4 tsp salt
- 4 tbsp unsalted butter, melted
- 1 tbsp white vinegar
- 1 tsp vanilla extract
- 4 large eggs, beaten

Instructions:

1. Preheat the oven to 350°F (175°C).
2. In a large bowl, combine sugar, cornmeal, flour, and salt.
3. Stir in melted butter, vinegar, vanilla, and beaten eggs.
4. Pour the mixture into the pre-baked pie crust.
5. Bake for 40-45 minutes, until the filling is set and golden on top.
6. Let the pie cool before serving.

Buttermilk Pie

Ingredients:

- 1 pre-baked pie crust (store-bought or homemade)
- 1 1/2 cups granulated sugar
- 1 tbsp all-purpose flour
- 1/4 tsp salt
- 3 large eggs, beaten
- 1 cup buttermilk
- 1 tsp vanilla extract
- 1/4 cup unsalted butter, melted

Instructions:

1. Preheat the oven to 350°F (175°C).
2. In a bowl, combine sugar, flour, and salt.
3. Stir in the eggs, buttermilk, vanilla extract, and melted butter.
4. Pour the mixture into the pie crust.
5. Bake for 45-50 minutes, until the center is set and slightly golden.
6. Let the pie cool before serving.

Apple Crumble Pie

Ingredients:

- 5 cups apples, peeled and sliced
- 3/4 cup granulated sugar
- 1/4 cup all-purpose flour
- 1/2 tsp ground cinnamon
- 1 tbsp lemon juice
- 1 pre-baked pie crust (store-bought or homemade)
- For the crumble topping:
    - 1/2 cup rolled oats
    - 1/3 cup all-purpose flour
    - 1/3 cup brown sugar
    - 1/4 cup unsalted butter, cold and cubed

Instructions:

1. Preheat the oven to 375°F (190°C).
2. In a bowl, toss the sliced apples with sugar, flour, cinnamon, and lemon juice.
3. Pour the apple mixture into the pre-baked pie crust.
4. In a separate bowl, combine oats, flour, brown sugar, and cold butter. Use a fork or pastry cutter to create a crumbly texture.
5. Sprinkle the crumble topping over the apples.
6. Bake for 45-50 minutes, until the topping is golden brown and the apples are tender.
7. Let the pie cool before serving.

Strawberry Pie

Ingredients:

- 4 cups fresh strawberries, hulled and sliced
- 1 cup granulated sugar
- 1/4 cup cornstarch
- 1/2 tsp vanilla extract
- 1 tbsp lemon juice
- 1 pre-baked pie crust (store-bought or homemade)

Instructions:

1. Preheat the oven to 375°F (190°C).
2. In a saucepan, combine 1/2 cup of sugar and cornstarch with 1/2 cup of water. Bring to a boil and cook until thickened.
3. Remove from heat and stir in vanilla extract and lemon juice.
4. Mix in the sliced strawberries.
5. Pour the strawberry mixture into the pre-baked pie crust.
6. Bake for 20-25 minutes until the filling is set.
7. Let the pie cool before serving.

Almond Cream Pie

Ingredients:

- 1 pre-baked pie crust (store-bought or homemade)
- 1/2 cup almond paste
- 1/2 cup heavy cream
- 1/2 cup whole milk
- 1/4 cup granulated sugar
- 2 large eggs, beaten
- 1/2 tsp vanilla extract

Instructions:

1. Preheat the oven to 350°F (175°C).
2. In a saucepan, heat cream and milk over medium heat until it just starts to simmer.
3. In a bowl, whisk together sugar, eggs, and almond paste until smooth.
4. Gradually add the hot cream mixture to the almond paste mixture, stirring constantly.
5. Pour the mixture into the pie crust.
6. Bake for 35-40 minutes, until the filling is set and golden on top.
7. Let the pie cool before serving.

Mincemeat Pie

Ingredients:

- 2 1/2 cups mincemeat (store-bought or homemade)
- 1 package of refrigerated pie crusts (or homemade pie crusts)
- 1 tbsp brandy or rum (optional)
- 1/2 tsp ground cinnamon
- 1/4 tsp ground nutmeg
- 1/4 tsp ground cloves

Instructions:

1. Preheat the oven to 375°F (190°C).
2. Roll out one pie crust and fit it into a 9-inch pie pan.
3. Fill with mincemeat, and sprinkle with cinnamon, nutmeg, and cloves.
4. Roll out the second pie crust and place it over the mincemeat. Trim excess dough and crimp the edges to seal.
5. Cut slits in the top crust to allow steam to escape.
6. Bake for 45-50 minutes, until the crust is golden brown.
7. Let the pie cool before serving.

Bourbon Pecan Pie

Ingredients:

- 1 pre-baked pie crust (store-bought or homemade)
- 1 1/2 cups pecan halves
- 3/4 cup light corn syrup
- 3/4 cup dark brown sugar
- 3 large eggs, beaten
- 1/4 cup unsalted butter, melted
- 2 tbsp bourbon
- 1 tsp vanilla extract
- 1/4 tsp salt

Instructions:

1. Preheat the oven to 350°F (175°C).
2. In a large bowl, whisk together corn syrup, brown sugar, eggs, melted butter, bourbon, vanilla extract, and salt.
3. Stir in the pecans and pour the mixture into the pie crust.
4. Bake for 45-50 minutes, until the filling is set and golden on top.
5. Let the pie cool before serving.

Nutella Pie

Ingredients:

- 1 pre-baked pie crust (store-bought or homemade)
- 1 cup Nutella
- 8 oz cream cheese, softened
- 1/2 cup powdered sugar
- 1/2 tsp vanilla extract
- 1 cup whipped cream or Cool Whip

Instructions:

1. In a large bowl, beat together Nutella, cream cheese, powdered sugar, and vanilla extract until smooth.
2. Fold in the whipped cream until well combined.
3. Pour the Nutella mixture into the pre-baked pie crust.
4. Refrigerate for at least 2 hours before serving.

Lemon Chess Pie

Ingredients:

- 1 pre-baked pie crust (store-bought or homemade)
- 1 1/2 cups granulated sugar
- 1 tbsp cornmeal
- 1 tbsp all-purpose flour
- 1/4 tsp salt
- 3 large eggs, beaten
- 1/4 cup unsalted butter, melted
- 1/4 cup lemon juice
- 1 tbsp lemon zest
- 1 tsp vanilla extract

Instructions:

1. Preheat the oven to 350°F (175°C).
2. In a bowl, combine sugar, cornmeal, flour, and salt.
3. Stir in eggs, melted butter, lemon juice, lemon zest, and vanilla extract until well combined.
4. Pour the filling into the pre-baked pie crust.
5. Bake for 40-45 minutes, until the center is set and golden.
6. Let the pie cool before serving.

Caramelized Pear Pie

Ingredients:

- 4 pears, peeled, cored, and sliced
- 1/2 cup granulated sugar
- 1 tbsp unsalted butter
- 1 tbsp lemon juice
- 1/4 tsp ground cinnamon
- 1/4 tsp ground ginger
- 1 tbsp cornstarch
- 1 pre-baked pie crust (store-bought or homemade)

Instructions:

1. Preheat the oven to 375°F (190°C).
2. In a skillet, melt butter over medium heat. Add pears and sugar, and cook until the pears are soft and caramelized, about 10 minutes.
3. Stir in lemon juice, cinnamon, ginger, and cornstarch. Cook for another 2 minutes until thickened.
4. Pour the pear mixture into the pre-baked pie crust.
5. Bake for 25-30 minutes, until the crust is golden and the filling is bubbling.
6. Let the pie cool before serving.

Mixed Berry Pie

Ingredients:

- 2 cups strawberries, hulled and sliced
- 1 cup blueberries
- 1 cup raspberries
- 1 cup blackberries
- 1 cup granulated sugar
- 1 tbsp cornstarch
- 1 tbsp lemon juice
- 1/2 tsp vanilla extract
- 1 pre-baked pie crust (store-bought or homemade)

Instructions:

1. Preheat the oven to 375°F (190°C).
2. In a bowl, toss all the berries with sugar, cornstarch, lemon juice, and vanilla extract.
3. Pour the berry mixture into the pre-baked pie crust.
4. Bake for 40-45 minutes, until the filling is thickened and the crust is golden brown.
5. Let the pie cool before serving.

Pear Ginger Pie

Ingredients:

- 5 pears, peeled, cored, and sliced
- 1/2 cup granulated sugar
- 1/4 cup brown sugar
- 2 tbsp cornstarch
- 1 tbsp grated fresh ginger
- 1 tbsp lemon juice
- 1/2 tsp ground cinnamon
- 1 pre-baked pie crust (store-bought or homemade)

Instructions:

1. Preheat the oven to 375°F (190°C).
2. In a bowl, combine the pears, granulated sugar, brown sugar, cornstarch, ginger, lemon juice, and cinnamon.
3. Pour the pear mixture into the pre-baked pie crust.
4. Bake for 40-45 minutes, until the crust is golden brown and the filling is thickened.
5. Let the pie cool before serving.

Pumpkin Praline Pie

Ingredients:

- 1 pre-baked pie crust (store-bought or homemade)
- 1 can (15 oz) pumpkin puree
- 3/4 cup heavy cream
- 1/2 cup granulated sugar
- 2 large eggs, beaten
- 1 tsp ground cinnamon
- 1/2 tsp ground nutmeg
- 1/2 tsp ground ginger
- 1/2 cup praline pecans, chopped
- 1/4 cup brown sugar

Instructions:

1. Preheat the oven to 350°F (175°C).
2. In a bowl, whisk together pumpkin puree, heavy cream, sugar, eggs, cinnamon, nutmeg, and ginger.
3. Pour the mixture into the pre-baked pie crust.
4. In a separate bowl, mix the praline pecans and brown sugar, then sprinkle on top of the pie.
5. Bake for 45-50 minutes, until the center is set and golden.
6. Let the pie cool before serving.

Cream Cheese Pumpkin Pie

Ingredients:

- 1 pre-baked pie crust (store-bought or homemade)
- 1 package (8 oz) cream cheese, softened
- 1 can (15 oz) pumpkin puree
- 3/4 cup granulated sugar
- 2 large eggs, beaten
- 1 tsp ground cinnamon
- 1/2 tsp ground ginger
- 1/4 tsp ground nutmeg
- 1/2 cup heavy cream

Instructions:

1. Preheat the oven to 350°F (175°C).
2. In a bowl, beat together cream cheese, pumpkin puree, sugar, eggs, cinnamon, ginger, and nutmeg until smooth.
3. Stir in the heavy cream and pour the mixture into the pie crust.
4. Bake for 45-50 minutes, until the pie is set and golden on top.
5. Let the pie cool before serving.

Apple Cranberry Pie

Ingredients:

- 4 cups apples, peeled and sliced
- 1 cup fresh cranberries
- 1 cup granulated sugar
- 2 tbsp all-purpose flour
- 1 tsp ground cinnamon
- 1 tbsp lemon juice
- 1 pre-baked pie crust (store-bought or homemade)

Instructions:

1. Preheat the oven to 375°F (190°C).
2. In a bowl, toss the apples, cranberries, sugar, flour, cinnamon, and lemon juice.
3. Pour the apple cranberry mixture into the pre-baked pie crust.
4. Bake for 45-50 minutes, until the crust is golden brown and the filling is bubbly.
5. Let the pie cool before serving.

Spiced Pear Pie

Ingredients:

- 5 pears, peeled, cored, and sliced
- 3/4 cup granulated sugar
- 1/4 cup brown sugar
- 1 tbsp cornstarch
- 1 tsp ground cinnamon
- 1/2 tsp ground ginger
- 1/4 tsp ground nutmeg
- 1 tbsp lemon juice
- 1 pre-baked pie crust (store-bought or homemade)

Instructions:

1. Preheat the oven to 375°F (190°C).
2. In a bowl, toss the pears with sugar, brown sugar, cornstarch, cinnamon, ginger, nutmeg, and lemon juice.
3. Pour the pear mixture into the pre-baked pie crust.
4. Bake for 40-45 minutes, until the crust is golden and the filling is bubbling.
5. Let the pie cool before serving.

Chocolate Silk Pie

Ingredients:

- 1 pre-baked pie crust (store-bought or homemade)
- 8 oz semi-sweet chocolate, chopped
- 3/4 cup heavy cream
- 3/4 cup powdered sugar
- 1 tsp vanilla extract
- 2 large eggs
- 1 tbsp unsalted butter, melted

Instructions:

1. In a small saucepan, heat the heavy cream over medium heat until it begins to simmer. Remove from heat and stir in the chopped chocolate until smooth.
2. In a separate bowl, whisk the eggs, powdered sugar, and vanilla extract until combined.
3. Add the egg mixture to the chocolate mixture and stir in melted butter.
4. Pour the filling into the pre-baked pie crust and refrigerate for at least 4 hours until set.
5. Top with whipped cream before serving.

Chocolate Hazelnut Pie

Ingredients:

- 1 pre-baked pie crust (store-bought or homemade)
- 1 cup Nutella or chocolate hazelnut spread
- 1/2 cup heavy cream
- 1/2 cup powdered sugar
- 2 large eggs, beaten
- 1 tsp vanilla extract
- 1/4 cup chopped hazelnuts, toasted

Instructions:

1. Preheat the oven to 350°F (175°C).
2. In a bowl, whisk together Nutella, heavy cream, powdered sugar, eggs, and vanilla extract until smooth.
3. Pour the mixture into the pre-baked pie crust.
4. Bake for 25-30 minutes until the filling is set.
5. Let the pie cool, then top with toasted hazelnuts before serving.

Pineapple Pie

Ingredients:

- 1 can (20 oz) crushed pineapple, drained
- 1/2 cup granulated sugar
- 1 tbsp cornstarch
- 1 tbsp lemon juice
- 1/2 tsp vanilla extract
- 1/4 tsp ground nutmeg
- 1 pre-baked pie crust (store-bought or homemade)

Instructions:

1. Preheat the oven to 375°F (190°C).
2. In a saucepan, combine pineapple, sugar, cornstarch, lemon juice, vanilla extract, and nutmeg. Cook over medium heat until the mixture thickens, about 5-7 minutes.
3. Pour the filling into the pre-baked pie crust.
4. Bake for 25-30 minutes, until the crust is golden and the filling is bubbly.
5. Let the pie cool before serving.

Apricot Pie

Ingredients:

- 4 cups fresh or canned apricots, sliced
- 1 cup granulated sugar
- 2 tbsp cornstarch
- 1 tbsp lemon juice
- 1/2 tsp ground cinnamon
- 1/4 tsp ground ginger
- 1 pre-baked pie crust (store-bought or homemade)

Instructions:

1. Preheat the oven to 375°F (190°C).
2. In a bowl, combine apricots, sugar, cornstarch, lemon juice, cinnamon, and ginger.
3. Pour the apricot mixture into the pre-baked pie crust.
4. Bake for 35-40 minutes, until the crust is golden and the filling is bubbly.
5. Let the pie cool before serving.

Coconut Lime Pie

Ingredients:

- 1 pre-baked pie crust (store-bought or homemade)
- 1 can (14 oz) sweetened condensed milk
- 1/2 cup sour cream
- 1/4 cup lime juice
- 1/2 cup shredded coconut
- 1 tsp lime zest
- 1/4 tsp vanilla extract

Instructions:

1. Preheat the oven to 350°F (175°C).
2. In a bowl, whisk together sweetened condensed milk, sour cream, lime juice, shredded coconut, lime zest, and vanilla extract.
3. Pour the mixture into the pre-baked pie crust.
4. Bake for 15-20 minutes, until the filling is set.
5. Let the pie cool, then refrigerate for at least 2 hours before serving.

Grapefruit Pie

Ingredients:

- 1 pre-baked pie crust (store-bought or homemade)
- 1 cup fresh grapefruit juice
- 1 tbsp grated grapefruit zest
- 1/2 cup granulated sugar
- 2 large eggs, beaten
- 1 tbsp cornstarch
- 1/2 cup heavy cream

Instructions:

1. Preheat the oven to 350°F (175°C).
2. In a saucepan, combine grapefruit juice, grapefruit zest, sugar, eggs, and cornstarch. Cook over medium heat until thickened, about 5-7 minutes.
3. Remove from heat and stir in heavy cream.
4. Pour the filling into the pre-baked pie crust.
5. Bake for 25-30 minutes, until the filling is set and the crust is golden.
6. Let the pie cool before serving.

Maple Pecan Pie

Ingredients:

- 1 pre-baked pie crust (store-bought or homemade)
- 1 cup maple syrup
- 1/2 cup granulated sugar
- 3 large eggs, beaten
- 1/4 cup unsalted butter, melted
- 1 tsp vanilla extract
- 1/2 tsp ground cinnamon
- 1/4 tsp ground nutmeg
- 1 1/2 cups pecan halves

Instructions:

1. Preheat the oven to 350°F (175°C).
2. In a bowl, whisk together maple syrup, sugar, eggs, melted butter, vanilla extract, cinnamon, and nutmeg.
3. Stir in the pecans and pour the mixture into the pre-baked pie crust.
4. Bake for 45-50 minutes, until the filling is set and the top is golden.
5. Let the pie cool before serving.

Mocha Cream Pie

Ingredients:

- 1 pre-baked pie crust (store-bought or homemade)
- 1 cup heavy cream
- 1/2 cup strong brewed coffee, cooled
- 1/2 cup granulated sugar
- 2 oz semi-sweet chocolate, chopped
- 1/2 tsp vanilla extract

Instructions:

1. In a saucepan, heat the heavy cream and brewed coffee until hot, but not boiling.
2. Add the chopped chocolate and sugar, stirring until melted and smooth.
3. Remove from heat and stir in vanilla extract.
4. Pour the mixture into the pre-baked pie crust and refrigerate for at least 4 hours until set.
5. Top with whipped cream before serving.

Apricot Almond Pie

Ingredients:

- 4 cups fresh apricots, pitted and sliced
- 1/2 cup granulated sugar
- 1/4 cup sliced almonds
- 2 tbsp cornstarch
- 1 tbsp lemon juice
- 1/2 tsp almond extract
- 1 pre-baked pie crust (store-bought or homemade)

Instructions:

1. Preheat the oven to 375°F (190°C).
2. In a bowl, combine apricots, sugar, sliced almonds, cornstarch, lemon juice, and almond extract.
3. Pour the mixture into the pre-baked pie crust.
4. Bake for 35-40 minutes, until the crust is golden and the filling is bubbling.
5. Let the pie cool before serving.

Plum Pie

Ingredients:

- 4 cups fresh plums, pitted and sliced
- 1 cup granulated sugar
- 1 tbsp lemon juice
- 1 tbsp cornstarch
- 1/2 tsp ground cinnamon
- 1 pre-baked pie crust (store-bought or homemade)

Instructions:

1. Preheat the oven to 375°F (190°C).
2. In a bowl, combine plums, sugar, lemon juice, cornstarch, and cinnamon.
3. Pour the mixture into the pre-baked pie crust.
4. Bake for 35-40 minutes, until the crust is golden and the filling is bubbly.
5. Let the pie cool before serving.

www.ingramcontent.com/pod-product-compliance
Lightning Source LLC
LaVergne TN
LVHW081505060526
838201LV00056BA/2950